SMALL DECISIONS
BIG IMPACT

Copyright © 2021 Stepping Stone Press LLC.

All rights reserved. No part of this book may be reproduced in any form without permission in writing from the publisher.

Printed in the United States of America

Hardback ISBN: 978-1-956582-01-7
Paperback ISBN: 978-1-956582-05-5
eBook ISBN: 978-1-956582-04-8

Dedicated to B.L.

SMALL DECISIONS **BIG IMPACT**

CONTENTS

The Introduction..9

GOALS
1. The Importance Of Understanding The Maze................17
2. Your Teachers Were Right...23
3. Blessed Beyond Belief..27
4. Waving Goodbye To The Pretty Girls............................33

FINANCIAL
5. Massive Moves Equals Massive Results.........................41
6. If It Scares You, It Might Be Good For You...................47
7. Listen Like You Give A F*ck..53
8. The Quest For Financial Freedom..................................61
9. Making Money While You Sleep....................................65

PATIENCE
10. Finding The Calm Within The Storm............................73
11. Exercise? I Thought You Said Extra Rice.......................79
12. There Is No Elevator To Success Just Stairs..................85
13. You Fail Only When You Stop Trying...........................91
14. The Art Of Patience...95

INVESTING

15. The Chapter You Will Most Likely Skip..................103
16. Making The World A Better Place........................109
17. Skip The E & Let It Go..................................117
18. Their Limits Not Yours..................................123
19. A GPS To Your Life Could Be Useful.....................129

GRIT

20. Striving To Be Better Than Yesterday 137
21. Surround Yourself With Greatness.......................143
22. Trust Your Struggle....................................149

THE
INTRODUCTION

Hey! My name is Michael Nhin. I'm a twenty-two-year-old college dropout. The idea of spending four or more years and a large sum of money to commit to a single career path was terrifying to me. I didn't have much experience with everything the world had to offer, so how was I supposed to decide what my life was going to revolve around? I followed everyone else to college because that's what society told me to do. It was strange to me that everyone around me knew exactly what they wanted to do for the rest of their lives. I never knew what I wanted for myself, and I didn't want anyone else to decide for me, so I dropped out of college.

What I do know is that I love helping others. So, I made this book to reach out to anyone and everyone who might be struggling to overcome an obstacle in their life. No matter how large or small the challenge is, I guarantee that this book will help you come closer to obtaining peace and happiness in your life.

The goal of this book is to provide you with a couple of ideas and stories. Ideas that will hopefully help you to live a happier and more meaningful life. Ideas that I have acquired from reading books and firsthand experiences. Perhaps not everything in this book will be helpful, but I can only hope that at least one of my chapters will reach out to you and help you to carve your own path in this world.

Before we start, I just want to say that I'm not some twenty-year-old millionaire dropout or something. I have had a couple of successes. More importantly, I feel as if I have some knowledge that others may not have had the chance to learn or might have forgotten. So, I'm here to share this knowledge or to help remind you of it.

I was about twenty years old when I realized I was inside this strange maze called life. I was working at my parents' restaurant five days a week, eleven hours a day, with the single thought of money. One night after a long day of work, I locked up the restaurant and sat outside. It was pitch-black, and my car was on the other side of the parking lot. I soon dazed off while looking at some trash that was left on the ground. Right above the trash were tiny bugs flying around, and then I wondered to myself if I was making the right decision?

Before this, I was studying at the University of Oklahoma. I decided to drop out after my freshman year. At the time I didn't know what I wanted to do with my life. I was stressing out. I was constantly being told how to live my life and that school was the only path. I was told that I needed to have my whole life planned out and to focus on a career. How does one make these decisions and life commitments if they don't know what they truly love doing? Society suggests that I need to go to college if I want any chance at success. My family and friends strongly disapproved as I turned my back on their "ideal" ways. After quitting college, I had all these negative thoughts for the following years. Thoughts such as, *What was I thinking? Why was I dropping out of college? What was I going to do with my life? How will I become someone who is successful? Who would ever want someone who didn't know what they were doing with their life? What if I don't have a chance at a family because I wouldn't be able to support one?* The negative thoughts were never-ending, but I soon learned many of my friends experienced similar thoughts. These thoughts flooded our heads during all hours of the day and night. Sometimes I still have these thoughts, and I'm certain my friends still have them as well.

One major obstacle I continually face is the thought of all my friends graduating without me. This mentally eats at me every day and has made me feel like a failure. Sometimes, when I stress about it too much, I start to have self-doubt. Have you ever felt like your world was crashing down and there was nothing you could do? This is how I feel and I'm positive everyone in the world at some point in his or her life will experience these feelings too. There is something you can do about it though, so I hope you stick around.

The Introduction

SMALL DECISIONS **BIG IMPACT**

GOALS

"Life is a maze. It has many twists and turns, but you can't get twisted up in the wrong turn."

-Samantha Villarreal

1

THE IMPORTANCE OF UNDERSTANDING
THE MAZE

Life is one ginormous f*cking maze. Let me tell you, I never knew it was until I read this book that my best friend, Ben, gave me. Back in my senior year of high school, I remember sitting in Ben's garage talking about life. This was someone I talked to about everything and anything with. That day, we were discussing our futures and what we didn't want to do with our lives. For example, we didn't want to work jobs that we dreaded with bosses who didn't care about us. We wanted to have a career that was enjoyable, even if we weren't paid well. A career that makes people want to jump out of bed and not feel like they were going to a miserable nine-to-five job was what we desired. Next, we discussed where we wanted to move to once we were happy with our careers. We didn't want to stay in Oklahoma once we became successful. We both agreed to move away from Oklahoma, even though this is where we grew up. Instead, we always agreed on living on a beach where it was always sunny and warm.

After dreaming about our futures, Ben asked me if I heard of something called the Rat Race. I glanced up at him with a confused look on my face and laughed. "Did you say, 'rat race'?" I asked him. He explained a portion of it before he quickly scurried into his house. A couple minutes later he returned with a book in hand and a huge grin on his face. He told me that someone important had given him this book and that he wanted me to read it. After flipping through, I decided it was an easy read, plus it had some pictures. At that time, I didn't really enjoy reading; however, he genuinely wanted me to read it. The next day I read it throughout school and easily finished. It was a great read. I would suggest picking it up, but the version Ben gave me was extremely old and the author's name had worn off. There are many modern versions of this book out there, perhaps try reading one when you have time.

The Maze, which is what I call the rat race, is basically a visual representation of how we constantly get so caught up in life. Imagine a maze with people walking around in it. They are all looking for the middle of the maze, which holds what they truly desire, a way out of the maze. We focus so much on money and work that we forget what it is we are chasing. We forget about all our dreams and goals that we want to achieve or create in our lifetime. Whether it is to write a book, become the president, or cure cancer. All those dreams and goals become lost in the shadows of the Maze over time. Why does this happen? Visualize yourself inside of the Maze, and with every turn and twist the Maze becomes deeper and more confusing. With each year you run around in the Maze, you soon grow weary and comfortable of the same paths presented in front of you. It doesn't have to be like that, though; with this book you'll be able to carve a path straight to the middle. It will take time. Your dreams and goals will soon be attainable if you are open to learning the material in this book.

Don't get caught up in what everyone else is doing. Don't follow a path because others tell you to. No matter how convincing someone is, know that they are not you and don't always know what's best for you. That is for you to figure out, so stop listening to the Chicken Littles. It is up to you to find out what path is going to lead you to a more fulfilling life.

So, always keep in mind the Maze when life gets confusing and overwhelming. Remember what exactly it is that you're chasing, and life will start to make sense again. It's okay to get lost at first, because that allows you to find out what you truly want. Carve through that damn Maze and find out who you were meant to be. Don't know where to start? What about with a goal?

The Importance Of Understanding The Maze

"A goal without a plan is just a wish."

-Antoine de Saint-Exupéry

YOUR TEACHERS
WERE RIGHT

Remember all those times in school when we had to write out our goals and *blah diblah blah*? We didn't enjoy it, nor did we want to do it—well, at least I didn't. It seems like our teachers and mentors were right after all, for making us practice goal setting. Ask any successful person in the world if they have goals. They will all tell you the same answer and that is *of course!* It doesn't matter how difficult or simple the goal is. If you have a goal, then there will be direction and motivation in life.

When I was fourteen, my goal was to earn enough money to buy my own Xbox. I wanted it so badly, but my parents told me they weren't going to buy it for me. So, I asked them what I should do. They told me that if I truly wanted it I could do chores or sell some of my stuff to make money. The Xbox I wanted was around $500 at the time, and I had nothing in my wallet. I actually didn't even have a wallet. It seemed like so much work, but I told myself I was going to get it. For weeks I washed dishes, cleaned the house, and sold random things like my collector basketball cards. After a month I had generated only $350. The thought of how much work I did compared to how much money I had obtained strongly discouraged me. I thought about giving up on my goal of buying an Xbox even though I was so close. I remember complaining to my mother about it taking too long and that I was never going to make it. Afterwards, she sat me down and told me to focus my goal and to use affirmations. She stated that I needed to remember what motivated me in the first place instead of wasting my energy being upset.

So, I dragged my feet into my room and stared at the wall. I started to feel sorry for myself, while I imagined all my friends having a blast without me on their Xboxs. What was my mother talking about? Of course, I was focusing on my goal! What in the world is an affirmation, anyways? I wasn't wasting my energy complaining, or was I? After a couple hours of thinking and googling, the thought really sank in. I took a couple deep breaths and told myself that I could do this. I was encouraged to achieve my goal once again. Two weeks later I had my Xbox, only to find out that all my friends were grounded from playing too much!

That was my first big goal that I had achieved, and since then, I believed I could do anything. Now, I know this sounded very childish. If you think about it though, is there any way you could relate to this? Have you ever come within arm's reach of your goal but quit because you were exhausted or discouraged? What about wasting your time and energy by complaining like I had done? You see, even though this story happened years ago, I know that I can still relate to it and use it no matter how old I become. There were many times when I wanted to give up writing this book because it was too time consuming and exhausting to reread over and over again. Then, I think back and realize all the work I have already put in and tell myself to stop being childish like when I was fourteen. No matter what your goal is or how unattainable it may seem, you'll never know what you can achieve if you first don't *start*. Whether it is a thought in your head, or maybe a goal you wrote down, starting is the first and hardest step.

"I am grateful for what I am and have. My thanksgiving is perpetual."

-Henry David Thoreau

BLESSED BEYOND
BELIEF

After purchasing my Xbox, I was hooked on it, like many of my friends were. When I began high school, however, my addiction to playing video games peaked. I would stay up all night and play it until I heard the birds chirping the next morning. After a few hours of sleep, I would then head off to school when my alarm was finished screaming at me. When I got home from school I would jump right back on my Xbox. My parents tried to discipline me, but I would always find a way to get back online. I was losing sleep, and my grades were falling lower than my parents' expectations. If you couldn't tell from my picture on the back of this book, I am Asian American. If you don't know the Asian grading system, I will educate you. If you received an A that meant "Average," B meant "Bad," C meant "Can't have dinner," D meant "Don't come home," and F meant "F*ck". My parents were infuriated with my academics. I remember being so scared that at one point I didn't go home after school. When I did return home, my parents did the unexpected. Instead of punishing me, they sat me down and encouraged me in a way I couldn't say no. For once, they offered to buy me a new car if I reached a goal of all straight A's for the rest of high school while keeping up with my extracurricular activities. During that time, I was participating in track, tennis, and cross-country.

Now, it was sophomore year in the second semester, and my grades had fallen to C's and B's. I thought it was going to be impossible to get my car. Not only did I have to take a sharp turnaround for the second semester, I also had to keep up the consistency for another two years. Because of my grades my parents decided to take away my Xbox and disconnect the Wi-Fi when I was home. That was okay with me, I focused on school and the thought of the car. The idea of my parents buying me something was a huge deal. I had always been taught that if I worked hard and saved my own money, I could buy whatever I wanted. So, anytime I received money I saved it all until I really wanted something. Eventually I was old enough to get a job. Then soon after I turned sixteen and bought a used car with all of my savings. So, the fact that my parents were offering to buy me something was extraordinary.

The thought of achieving straight A's for another two years was overwhelming. To reduce some of my anxiety, I told myself that I would just focus on the remaining of the semester. After that semester was over, I was exhausted. Turning those grades around in such a short span of time was difficult. However, the late nights and extra credits I asked for paid off.

Now, all that stood in my way was another two years. Once again, I was starting to feel overwhelmed. I often reminded myself of how I bought my own Xbox and how simple my struggle actually was compared to how difficult I was making it. I stopped complaining about being exhausted and focused on the big picture. I gave myself positive affirmations daily even though it felt silly. I told myself that I could do it and the goal now was to take it day by day. I would focus on each test and assignment individually instead of facing the stress of the two years as a whole. That's when I truly learned the importance of breaking up goals into smaller increments. If I hadn't broken the years up into increments, I'm almost positive that I would have given up from being too stressed out.

Two extremely long years later, I graduated from Edmond Memorial High School with my straight A's and moved to Norman to attend the University of Oklahoma. That's when I could finally collect my prize. Was I going to acquire a new blacked-out Jeep or a sports car? My parents sat me down and told me my options. *My options? What were they talking about? Was I not going to get a new car after I worked so hard?* They gave me two options. They said I could receive a new car like we had agreed or I had the opportunity to invest that money into my first piece of real estate. They told me to think about my decision and that they would be happy to give me either of the two for working so hard and achieving my goal.

I remember the first time I saw the property that my parents deemed a great investment. The house was covered in graffiti, the windows were broken, and it smelled like something, or someone, had died inside of it. I thought to myself how frightening the house was and that I knew I was for sure going to choose a new car. In my head, I had this image of myself cruising around in my brand-new shiny Jeep with my friends and a bunch of girls. Like, I had twenty girls in my Jeep with the music blasting from my subwoofers. Keep in mind at this point in my life I was eighteen and still wanted to be Mr. Popular. So, why would I want a property that I would have to spend my whole summer fixing up, and on top of that, I would have to invest more of my own money into? Money that I didn't even have yet! Later, I learned that my parents were giving me this option for a reason. After reflecting, I realized that I didn't need a new car. I just wanted one for the wrong reasons. I mean, I did have a used car already that I had purchased myself, and it was still working, so why did I need a new car?

The truth is that you may not have the opportunity like I had. I was blessed that my parents taught me how to be persistent and hardworking. They were preparing me for the hardships of life and to not quit when the going gets tough. They were constantly teaching me so many different lessons that I didn't even realize. We then had one last discussion before I made my decision. That's when I learned about delayed gratification.

"The lure of your long-term satisfaction must be greater than the lure of your short-term gratification."

-Tony Curl

4

WAVING GOODBYE TO THE
PRETTY GIRLS

What the hell is delayed gratification? This term applies when someone resists the temptation of an immediate reward in preference for a later reward. For example, telling a child they can have one cookie right now, but if they wait one whole hour, then they can have five cookies. There was an actual study done that was somewhat like this example, it was called the Marshmallow Test. This test was conducted in 1972 by a psychologist, Walter Mischel. In this study they examined the correlation between the children's choices to the jobs they received later in life. As those children grew older, the ones who waited for one more hour ended up proceeding to better jobs, compared to the children who didn't want to wait. A little something to think about the next time you're presented with two options.

Now, even though I wanted a new car to show off to my friends, there was something else I wanted even more. There is a term that I reluctantly heard around my house all the time. That term is financial freedom. Even to this day it's still in the back of my head, and it always affects my decision-making for the better. Financial freedom, in a nutshell, is a place in life when you are no longer stressed about money and feel at peace with any liabilities. We will get to this later in the book. Delayed gratification and financial freedom both go hand in hand with one another. If you didn't grow up hearing these terms, then hopefully I can instill them in you. After thinking about these two terms that my parents had drilled into my head, I knew what I desired. I said no to the shiny car and the pretty girls. I decided to focus on investing and fixing up my first house.

This house, in the long run, will prove more worthwhile than the other option. Investing in this broken-down house meant I would have to work the whole summer before going off to college. Strangely, I knew that this was what I wanted. I knew that after the house was finished, if leased, would bring me a steady monthly income. This would allow me to focus my energy elsewhere while still making money. This was something that I could keep and receive income from until I choose to sell it. Although, it might take six years for the house to pay for itself, everything after that would be pure profit. Real estate is often referred to as the old man's game of delayed gratification.

Another example of delayed gratification comes from one of my closest friends, Madison. She told me recently that she was going to stay in college an extra couple of years. Holy sh*t, my worst nightmare. She could easily graduate whenever she wanted to and secure a well-paying job; however, she aims to be better than the average Joe. She told me that everyone has that "well-paying" job, but she didn't want to be like the everyone else. She is pushing herself to stay in school and to take all these hard classes; she is giving herself a chance at her dream job. I'm not sure about you, but I believe it takes a strong understanding of delayed gratification to want to stay in school for another couple years. Madison understands the commitment, struggle, pressure, and money it will take to have a chance at her dream job. Yet, she continues to persevere because this is her main goals.

Everyone will aim towards different goals and experience different types of delayed gratification. Here are some simple steps to follow for when you want to strive for delayed gratification.

1. Plan on how you will achieve your goal.

You will need to specifically write out your plan with the steps necessary to achieve your goals. Say your goal is to purchase a car or home. Maybe the first thing you need to do is acquire a job. Then, you need to calculate the number of hours you will work a week. Finally, write down how long you will need to work to make enough money to purchase this car or home.

2. Take your goal and break it up into increments.

Set miniature goals for each month and how much money will need to be saved. Maybe the car you want is $10,000. If you were to save all your money all the time, you might overwhelm yourself. So, set aside a little amount to save each month and leave yourself extra money to spend on other things such as food or fun.

3. Identify alternative rewards.

In this step say you're trying to save money by not going to the bars so much with your friends. Every time you successfully do this, reward yourself with something small that doesn't cost too much money. For example, maybe reward yourself by renting a movie at home that you've been wanting to watch. The movie will act as a reward but won't cost nearly as much if you went out to the bars.

4. Use positive affirmations.

Positive affirmations are statements that you say to yourself when you're trying to overcome obstacles. Try not to sabotage yourself with negative thoughts when you become stressed out from all the hard work. Tell yourself: "You can do this" or "You've got this"!

There are so many benefits from learning about delayed gratification. What is something that you could achieve from practicing delayed gratification? Is it that summer body that you have always wanted? Maybe you're swapping all those fast-food meals that are so convenient for a home-cooked meal that is cheaper and healthier? It could be skipping nights out with your friends to save money for your first house. Maybe it's not taking a vacation in order to pay off your student loans. In my case it was skipping summers with my friends to grow and learn these things I'm trying to relay to you. It could be anything—just remember to think if your decisions are bringing you closer or further away from your goals. Practice delayed gratification with small goals, and gradually you will start to achieve more and more until it becomes a habit of understanding this term. Once you practice this long enough, take your goal and multiple it by ten.

SMALL DECISIONS **BIG IMPACT**

FINANCIAL

"Shoot for the moon. Even if you miss, you'll land among the stars."

    -Oscar Wilde

MASSIVE MOVES EQUALS
MASSIVE RESULTS

Who wants to be a millionaire? I guess the real question is: Who doesn't want to be a millionaire? One of my goals, as of this very moment, is to be a millionaire by the time I'm twenty-five. Now, money does not buy happiness, however, it does relieve a great deal of stress compared to not having enough. If you don't have enough money to live how you want then you might experience frustration, depression, or pain.

If you haven't read the book *The 10X Rule* by Grant Cardone, I highly recommend it. The overall message of the book is to have a goal in mind, then multiply it by ten. This idea will then propel you to take major action in order to achieve your set goal. Action that would not have been taken but set aside forever if not for this rule!

When I read *The 10x Rule*, at first, I thought the idea was insane. Initially my goal was to obtain $100,000 by twenty-five, but that was when I was twenty. I remember thinking to myself that if I kept working at my current job, then I would reach the goal by the time I'm twenty-three. After reading that book, I realized that I was crippling myself by setting a goal that comfortable.

The book told me to aim high, and even if I did not reach my goal, I would still finish better than what I initially visualized. Setting low goals is what people do when they want to stay in their comfort zone and not really challenge themselves for something they truly desire. So instead of $100,000 by twenty-five, it was going to be a million. I gave myself a massive goal and I subconsciously pushed myself to make massive moves. After writing about this in my journal, I smashed my initial goal by a little more than double and I'm only twenty-two right now. So, instead of sitting there and being comfortable with the idea that I was going to reach $100,000 within the next four years, I went out and found a way to get massive results.

Instead of working only to save my money, I thought to myself, *How could I make my money work for me?* So, I invested what I had made from my jobs into another piece of real estate. My father had found a house in Oklahoma City that one of his friends were selling. It was cheap, but for a reason. The property needed to be totally redone, just like the first house I invested in. Believe it or not, this one was much worse. It had broken windows, the stench of death, a bunch of junk inside, and all sorts of rodents running around. On top of all that, a good portion of the inside was burned by a fire and had not been touched in years. At the time I didn't know it was going to cost me two years of paychecks and all the income from my first house.

In addition, I would need to be working on the house during my free time since I didn't have the money to pay for workers. I had to wake up and go straight to the house to work during my off days from my actual job. After working on the house for eight hours, I would go straight home to sleep. Then, when I woke up, I would do it all over again with the thought of being a millionaire in the back of my head. I kept striving for that goal no matter the condition of the weather. I had to fight through the hot summer days with all of the mosquitoes and sweat. Then face the freezing rainy nights of winter. I wanted it so badly that I worked on the property like a maniac! Sure, at times I got discouraged and even angry, but I kept reminding myself of my goal. All that ambition and sheer will would not have appeared if it were not for that book by Grant Cardone. If I had not multiplied my goal by ten, then I guarantee that I would have been wasting my time playing video games on my off time. I would still be going to work and telling people that I was "comfortable" with my life. I would be waiting for my initial goal of $100,000 to come to me instead of making something happen myself!

There are two reasons why people believe they can't do something.

1. The people around them tell them that they can't.

2. They succumb to their own negative thoughts when they need to do the opposite.

Do you ever have tiny, annoying voices of doubt in the back of your head? It constantly tells you that you can't do something, even though you know you can. Yeah, don't let this self-doubt boss you around. Have faith in yourself instead of listening to the self-doubt or voices of other people who are scared.

So, once again it's time to take a step back and try to apply this method to one of your goals. What would happen if you multiplied one of them by ten? There is no telling what you could achieve if you challenge yourself to be great. Make massive goals and you will push yourself in ways you can't even imagine. If you have trouble or question your strength, then practice the steps I listed about delayed gratification. Making the 10X rule a habit in your life might just change it for the better. Even if it scares you, I suggest embracing it.

"Run towards your fears. Embrace them. On the other side of your greatest fears lives your greatest life."

-Robin Sharma

IF IT SCARES YOU, IT MIGHT BE
GOOD FOR YOU

Hey, good to see you're still here. I guess some of the stuff I'm blabbering about is interesting. Here is another idea that I believe is highly important to keep in mind. Do things that make you uncomfortable. Now, I'm not telling you to jump out of a plane or ride that scary roller coaster with all the ups, downs, and spins. (I still throw up every time on that thing, and no, they are not just for children). I'm talking about doing things that will help you grow more as a person and expand your abilities. Take a leap out of your comfort bubble! Embrace public speaking, or offer yourself up for that job promotion, even if it's out of your comfort zone. Seek those fears out and soon you will become a better version of yourself. Become that version of yourself that you only dreamed to be. Feed your brain with learning new things while pushing your limits. Yes,

I know it's scary, but the more you embrace fear, the more open you will be to new ideas. Embracing fear will help you in the future when you're forced to adapt to new ways. Trust me.

For example, let's talk about the restaurant industry. If you haven't noticed, more and more restaurants are teaming up with delivery services. Restaurants are picking this idea up because the market is headed in that direction and they don't want to be left behind. People are always so busy; it is more convenient for people to just order from home. Sometimes people just want to have their favorite foods delivered right to their door. I would be lying if I said I haven't done this. Imagine if McDonald's said no to being open about change, if they didn't embrace this fear. I guarantee that a great amount of their business would've disappeared. When delivery services started becoming popular, it was terrifying for business owners. It was unknown and raised concerns about how it would affect their businesses. Now, these places are thriving, and they are able reach a whole new untapped source of consumers. Some restaurants embraced the fear while others avoided it. Those restaurants that avoided these delivery services are now having a delayed start and may have lost business because of that fear.

Here is an example of when I had to embrace my fear when I couldn't avoid it any longer. While growing up, I was a pretty shy kid who didn't talk much. Like most, I strongly disliked public speaking and would skip any class that required presentations. Then came the time when I couldn't avoid them anymore.

The moment I accepted a management position at my parents' restaurant was the moment I could not avoid public speaking any longer. As a manager I had to produce and provide meetings for my staff every month. In these meetings I had to present my ideas on how to guide and support my team to grow as individuals. When I first started hosting these meetings, it was frightening. Then, I thought about how I shouldn't have skipped all those classes in school. I was thrown to the wolves. Many of my employees were older than me, which only resulted in me being even more nervous.

The day finally came where I had to present at my first meeting as the manager. I had eleven more hours before we closed and that would be when the meeting began. The only thing I could do was practice the outline of the meeting in my head. When we closed the store, everyone gathered at a table and waited. I passed out my meeting outlines and everyone's eyes beamed toward me. I couldn't speak for a second. There was this huge amount of weight on my chest. When I did get words to come out, they were no more than a whisper. For now, let's just say the meeting was a success and I killed it. It was the best meeting in all of management history! Fist bumps all around! I wish it went like that. I remember at one point

I started sweating, which made me whisper even more. This had been my first meeting I ever conducted. I was nineteen years old. The thing is, with time, like everything else, my skills began to sharpen into tools for a better life. I soon realized that I started to look forward to teaching and speaking to my staff after I overcame my fear. Forcing myself into this uncomfortable situation helped me in more ways than I could even imagine. I'm an introvert, but, after embracing that fear I learned to be more of the person I only dreamed to be.

With my newfound courage, at my next job I wasn't scared to speak in front of all these strangers. My fear about speaking publicly has subsided tremendously. I'm not the best at speaking, but I can tell you that I've come a long way. Now I find myself constantly seeking out chances to place myself into uncomfortable situations. When my manager at work asks me to do something new, I don't question how difficult it is or what it is. I say, "Of course," and soon after, I end up learning something new that I can add to my skills portfolio. Retrospectively, if I hesitated or asked too many questions, then the job could have gone to another person, and I would not have had the chance to learn.

I cannot emphasize enough about the importance of embracing fear; I can only encourage you to trust me. Experiment with something small, then work your way up to the point where you will say yes to every opportunity that crosses your path. Don't hesitate and watch all these opportunities fade away because you are scared! You will never know your full potential if you don't try new things. So, after you finish reading this book, I want you to think about these words when you see an opportunity floating away. Are you willing to test my advice and become a better version of yourself? Let's see how well you were listening.

"We have two ears and one mouth so that we can listen twice as much as we speak."

-Epictetus

7

LISTEN LIKE YOU GIVE A F*CK

Don't skip this chapter just because it sounds simple. This idea might be the hardest one to practice. Learning to give your full attention to someone when they are trying to teach you something can be difficult. Not everyone has time to explain something more than once, nor do they want to. That is why learning to listen efficiently will be worth your time. People will come and go throughout your life, and it will be your choice whether you hear their advice or not.

Have you ever tried to explain something to someone, but they couldn't comprehend what you were saying? Then, you started to get upset? This happens to me all the time when I try to teach my little brothers anything. My brothers will always ask for help when they don't know how to do something, but they never want to listen to my advice. Of course, I teach them how to do it, but then they ask me the same questions the following week. To my brothers, learning to make and post a video on YouTube is only exciting after they post it. They enjoy the likes, views, and comments from everyone, but everything before that they choose not to learn. It came to the point where I told them I wasn't going to keep teaching them how to make videos because I have taught them so many times already. So, instead of taking the time to really process what I was teaching them, they had to take their time to relearn by themselves.

You're a very busy person. Imagine if someone asked for your advice, only to simply ask you the same questions the following week. No one wishes this upon himself or herself, so practice becoming the best listener you can be.

Now, when you're listening to others my only concern I have for you is to be careful of whom you listen to. There will be situations where you need to ask yourself, is this person giving you advice and thinking of your best interest? Believe it or not, there are people out there who will go out of their way to set you back. Perhaps it's because they don't want you to succeed, or maybe they envy you.

When people need something, no matter who they are, you'll be surprised to see what great lengths someone will go through to acquire it. Not only will these people consume your time, but they will also drain you mentally. Everyone has an opinion or advice that they believe is the right answer. There might not always be correct answers to your situation. So, choose wisely of whom you listen to. When you do find the right advice to listen to, there is no telling how far it will propel in life. To this day, I'm still practicing and learning to be a more diligent listener.

The day I truly realized it was significant to learn this trait was when I met a wise man who had also written his own book. It was a Friday night at the restaurant, and we were slammed. I was training a new cashier, dealing with an ice machine problem and doing sushi because one of our sushi chefs was out sick. That was when the man walked in and examined the restaurant. He seemed like an ordinary person, but when he walked up to the register, he started asking the cashier questions about the restaurant. Of course, the cashier didn't know the answers because it was only her third night working, so I stepped in.

At first, he asked me questions that I was able to answer effortlessly. Eventually, he asked me something that made me freeze for a second. The question totally threw me off when he asked, "Why are you working here?" Bewildered I replied, "Because I need the money?" He then proceeded to ask *why* to all my responses until we got to the point where I didn't have the answers anymore. His questions became more personal instead of relating to the restaurant, which is why I couldn't answer. "Why do you want your own business?" I took a breath, looked up into space, and thought, *Why did I want my own business?* He then casually walked away when I couldn't answer his question.

After he finished his dinner, he left the restaurant and returned with a book in his hands. He walked straight up to me and handed it to me. He told me that he wrote the book and wanted me to read it. The book sat in my bedroom untouched for two weeks until I decided to finally pick it up. I had no idea that this man was so successful until I had finished his book.

Fast-forward to a year later. For some reason I couldn't let go of the short conversation I had with that man. So, I decided to find answers. I have never really sought anyone out before. It was quite terrifying, but I figured, what was the worst that could happen? On the back of his book he had a phone number printed. I decided to give it a call but had no luck. After some research, I eventually found his business. On his company's website, I found his email address. My fears of being turned down hovered over my shoulders again.

Before I could think any longer, or convince myself not to, I sent him an email. I wasn't sure if he would receive it or a coworker would. To my surprise, he responded the next day to my email. He said, "Of course, I remember you. Call this number and we will set up a time to meet." I called the number and he answered immediately. I was not prepared, so I started sweating because I didn't know what to say. All the words that came out of my mouth were quiet. I felt like a fool. After a long, awkward conversation, he told me that I should come shadow him at his business. I said yes without even taking a second to think about it.

After speaking to him on the phone, I started questioning what I had just done. I didn't even know this man, yet I agreed to shadow him. Soon the what-ifs began to pop up in my head. *What if he is lying to me about who he is? What if I am just wasting my time? What if he doesn't help me? What if he asks me more questions that I don't have the answers to? What if I make a bigger fool out of myself?* The list of what-ifs went on and on. At this point, my fear of what I was doing peaked.

The day came when we agreed to meet. I had no idea what was going to happen or what I was even doing honestly. I showed up with an open ear until I learned more about who this man was. That shadowing experience turned out to be an unforgettable one. Here are just a few things I learned from that experience after realizing that this man was someone I wanted to really listen to. I learned that overcoming my fears pays off. I learned that my problems are nothing compared to those who are really suffering. What I want in life is much more than what I originally thought. This stranger is an extremely successful man. Not only does he live a successful life, but more importantly, a fulfilling one. As you can see this was not your typical shadowing. Because of this stranger, I decided that I will have a fulfilling life like he does. I know that the time I spent shadowing him will stick with me for the rest of my life.

You never know when you'll meet someone extraordinary who has been in the same exact position you're in. Pay attention to those you trust; these people take time out of their days to teach you something because they genuinely want to help. If I hadn't listened to what Tom was asking me and questioned it, I would not have learned those valuable lessons. If not for him, I would still be a robot who was just punching in and clocking out for money. That is when I realized I had become lost in the Maze. He made me take a step back and remember something without needing to ask me directly. To this day, I wonder how often I would still be running around in the Maze if I hadn't met him at the restaurant. At the time, I had been working so much that all I thought about was money. I longed for my own business and to be wealthy, but I wanted to word it differently which is why I paused on his last question. So, Tom, to answer your last "why", I want to become financially free and then help others achieve this milestone of freedom as well.

"Being rich is having money; being wealthy is having time."

    -Margaret Bonnano

THE QUEST FOR
FINANCIAL FREEDOM

The term financial freedom, in a nutshell, is a place in life when you are no longer stressed about money and feel at peace to make your own decisions. When I say that, what comes to mind? For some people they might think about being able to afford everything they ever dreamed of. For others, maybe it's the aspect of not worrying about how to pay for things they need. Sometimes the thought of not having to plan about saving for months or taking out a loan is what people want. Maybe you don't want to be intimidated by questions such as *Will I be able to pay my rent if purchase this car? Will I have enough money for a new windshield after paying the bills?* Perhaps you always wanted to buy new tires for your car but never had the money to do it. By being financially free, you could buy those tires without having to worry about a payment plan.

Others dream of financial freedom because they think about quitting their current job for one they actually love. Even if it means they will receive a smaller salary or less pay. They would have this luxury to make this decision because they are financially comfortable and can afford the downgrade in pay. Who wouldn't want to be financially free and do what they love every day?

I always thought financial freedom was the same thing as being called "rich". When I used that term *rich*, I found myself thinking about buying everything in the world. Most of which were things that I did not need. Such as numerous luxurious cars, helicopters, and mansions. Mentally, I kept having this dream. Then I changed my wording from being rich to financially free; it made me start to think about better ways to utilize my money.

When I think about what financial freedom means to me now, I imagine myself on a bright sunny day with clear skies being as happy as a child on Christmas Day. I find myself thinking about more ways to invest my money instead of going hog wild with it. Another thought when I think about financial freedom is giving back to those who helped me along this journey. Then inspire others to achieve their goals as well.

By simply wording my thoughts and goals differently, I think about more than just being rich. Striving to be financially free made me think about my family, goals, and steps on how to ultimately reach financial freedom. Now that you understand the term, what does it mean to you?

Realizing and defining what financial freedom is on your terms will help motivate you day-in and day-out. After you figure out what financial freedom means to you, then you will start questioning how you will obtain it. Contemplate if you manage your money correctly. Managing your money is a necessary skill to learn if you want to achieve financial freedom. Determine how much money needs to be put into the bank and how much money needs to be set aside for bills, rent, and food. Then there is also the money that needs to be set aside to spend as you wish. Without balance when handling your money, you become vulnerable and invite chaos to ruin your finances. You obviously can't spend all your money on useless things or only save your money. If you do one or the other, you might drive yourself mad. Find a balance and stick with a routine of handling your money. Once you do, you'll be closer to finding financial freedom! After you figure out how to manage your money, the next step is finding that money sitting in your bank could be working for you!

"If you don't find a way to make money while you sleep, you will work until you die."

-Warren Buffett

MAKING MONEY WHILE
YOU SLEEP

Have you ever wanted to make money while sleeping? What if I told you that you could and it's f*cking fantastic? It's called passive income. By building your passive income, you will be able to do this. Warren Buffett stated it best, "If you don't find a way to make money while you sleep, you will work until you die". This is how the financially fit stay wealthy. They make money work for them while the poor work for money. If you don't have any passive income, then how will you expect to achieve financial freedom? Ask yourself what is putting money in your pockets and what is taking money out? Passive income should be putting money into your pockets without making you have to work hard. Your mode of passive income should be received on a regular basis from some type of investment. These investments can be from residential properties, stocks, business, etc. I'm currently receiving about $4,000 in passive income each month from investing in stocks and real estate.

No one knows how long he or she has on this Earth. Time is your most valuable resource. Take a step back to see how you spend your days and decide if you are utilizing your precious time wisely. Without this passive income in your life, it is quite difficult to buy back your time. What do I mean by buying back your time? It's simple. When you have multiple streams of passive income, this will create more time for you to do the things you love. What if I had ten rental properties and made a monthly passive income amount of about $10,000 from them? I believe that if this were the case, then I would be spending more of my time writing this book instead working on it after work when I'm exhausted. Imagine all the things you could focus on if you acquired more passive income. If your passive income becomes large enough, there won't be a need to follow a work schedule. You could choose to be independent and make your own schedule. So, try investing in something that will help you gain passive income instead of buying materialistic things. In the long run it will be worth your time.

There are a large variety of investments you could choose from, but the most important thing is that you choose an investment *wisely*. Make sure to do research and seek advice for your investment before you start investing willy-nilly. The worst thing you could do is make a bad investment that you can't take back.

If I were going to invest in another residential property, I would need to do proper research before I purchase it. *Does the property need work done on it? If so, then how much would the work cost? Is the property in a good spot for the price being asked? Does this property have any liens or loans taken out on it that have not been paid for?* Not only can you lose your money in a bad investment, but you will also lose your time. No matter how great something seems, just remember that there is no going back in time to change your decisions.

What type of questions could you ask yourself before you make an investment? Think of at least ten questions and write them down. Questions about the time, money, and overall health of the investment. After doing so, try bouncing your ideas off someone you trust to see what he or she thinks of it. Like always, be careful whom you trust! Always be open to listening to someone even if you believe they can't help. You never know where you're going to hear an idea that you can build from.

For me, this book is another form of passive income. What if I told you that I'm the oldest of my siblings, yet it was my fourteen-year-old brother who convinced me to write this book? Would you believe me? "It's simple," he stated. "I just finished writing a children's book and it was so easy. You should try writing a book." That was all he had to say for the idea of writing a book to be planted into my head. I asked myself questions on whether this was a good idea for me, but I figured that if my little brother could do it, then so could I. Plus, I remember how much I enjoyed writing when I was college and *boom!* Now I'm writing my first book ever and this will help contribute to my passive income portfolio. Of course, after writing this book, I will need to market it. After that, however, I won't have to do much! Say I got it on Amazon, then I could be receiving a check every month while they sold my book!

Another way of obtaining passive income is by renting out a room in your house. My friend Justin makes passive income by doing this. Who knew? My friend studied this concept after going on vacation and realizing there is a market for it. He found himself not wanting to rent out a hotel room because it was too expensive. He also didn't trust most of them. Justin eventually found a room for rent online on Airbnb. On this web page he was able to read about the family renting the room out. He also read reviews about other people's experiences staying there. Along with that, Justin saw that the family provided breakfast, lunch, and dinner for guests who didn't want to cook during their stay. Renting the room had so many positives, and it was still cheaper than the hotel room; he couldn't believe it. When he returned home, that's when Justin decided to think about if this was a good source of passive income for him. After he figured he wasn't using the second bedroom in his house, he decided why not make money from it since it was empty? Now, Justin is making an extra $1,000 a month and has the chance to meet people from all around the world.

There are so many ways to make passive income. Hopefully, after reading this, I sparked some interest in the whole passive income talk. Maybe you're interested in writing a book or renting out a room in your house. I tell people all the time how rewarding it is to make money work for you instead of the opposite way around. It surprises me how many people are unaware of this concept and that it is possible for them. Now, I'm not going to lie to you. Building passive income is going to take a large amount of time and effort. It didn't take me a week or a month to write this book, nor will it take you a small amount of time to save up for an investment. You will be pushed to your limits, but you'll need to understand that there must be a balance. You obviously can't spend all your money on useless things, or just save all your money. If you do one or the other, you might drive yourself mad. Find a balance and stick with a routine of handling your money.

SMALL DECISIONS **BIG IMPACT**

PATIENCE

"I've learned that you can't have everything and do everything at the same time."

-Oprah Winfrey

10

FINDING THE CALM WITHIN
THE STORM

"I can't do it anymore. I work my butt off day in and day out and I don't see the point to it all. Is this all my life will ever be?" This is what you will sound like without balance. An imbalance could be physical, spiritual, or emotional. It's important to make the decision to create a more balanced life every single day. For me, the biggest problem I have with balance is working. I tend to find myself overworking.

At multiple points in my life, I worked three jobs simultaneously. There were multiple times where I had to rush from one job to the other because my schedules would overlap. It was difficult to keep up and I became drained. Soon I realized that after six months, I had to let one job go. Letting one of my jobs go may have extended the time to reach one of my personal goals; however, it saved my sanity. Even after leaving one of my jobs, I continued to feel overwhelmed. I was working harder than when I had three jobs because I put in more hours at the other two jobs. You can't just go full-blown work mode and expect everything to be fine like I did. You will burn out sooner or later, and it will be difficult to stay consistent after a burnout. There is a fine line between grinding and driving yourself into complete exhaustion. There must be balance in your life. That balance is something you will have to figure out to succeed with any long-term goals.

You can work for a better future but be sure to enjoy life when you can. What I'm saying is when you find yourself with some time away from work, really soak it in and breathe. Allow yourself time to think about how lucky you are. Be thankful for little things like your health, family, a roof over your head, or even clean water. Thinking about what you are grateful for when you have time will not only help encourage you to be more proactive, but it will make you more appreciative. When you are more appreciative you are happier and healthier. If this sounds silly or is something that you wouldn't normally do, you should be doing it now because you embrace fear! Try it, and if it helps, then you learned something new about yourself. If it doesn't, then it is not a big deal! Maybe it doesn't work because you need something more substantial and relaxing.

Try planning a trip with your family or friends as a reward for completing a milestone of one of your goals.

Everyone is different, and it is up to you to find your own balance. When finding your balance, be cautious not to do anything that could be dangerous to your time and work. I learned that the hard way when I would work all week and then party all weekend with my friends at the bars. I used to dread Mondays because I was so hung over and worn out. It would take me days to recover, and I could see in my work that I was sluggish and sloppy. All my motivation was lost. By the time I recovered, it was already the next weekend. This vicious cycle would happen over and over again. Don't get me wrong, I'm not saying you can't go out and drink with your friends. I'm just saying you need to find your balance. If you're reading this and can relate, then perhaps try stepping back to ponder whether you're overdoing it or not. Is it necessary to go out every day each weekend? There are other things to do with your time that don't result in raging hangovers every morning. Try spending your Sundays with your family or taking your dog to the park for once.

Don't think I'm just some goody two-shoes kid who just kisses ass either. I can "turn up" when I want to! Man, I sound old. The thing is, I just find my future more compelling than spending all my money and time at the bar on the weekends. After realizing how catastrophic I was being towards my goal, I tried changing my mindset and picked up better habits. One of my favorite habits is working out.

Finding The Calm Within The Storm

"Take care of your body. It's the only place you have to live."

-Jim Rohn

11

EXERCISE? I THOUGHT YOU SAID
EXTRA RICE

Eating some Hot Cheetos in bed sounds magnificent and all, but if your metabolism hasn't crapped out already, consider these next few sentences a warning. As you grow older, your metabolism usually slows down. This happens because your muscle mass decreases and your fat tends to increase. This, in turn, decreases the number of calories your body burns resulting in people becoming overweight and suffering from the negative effects of obesity. Here are a few negative effects of obesity: self-doubt, depression, anxiety, heart disease, and diabetes. We are given only one body and life, so shouldn't we take care of it? That's why I have made working out a lifestyle.

I don't care who you are or how simple your workout is, working out is incredible for your health. Even if you already work out, I will still recommend you read this chapter because it doesn't hurt to be reminded. People often think of working out to be exhausting and downright terrible. They see it more as a chore rather than a life choice. Working out can be so much more though! It doesn't matter how far you are running or how much you are lifting. It's the fact that you are making the time to be a healthier version of yourself, even though all the craziness that is happening in your life. The first few weeks or even months might be painful and tiring, but you will soon notice why people stick with it.

There is a point when a habit transforms into a lifestyle. It is truly unexplainable. It is something you must experience yourself. That point is when you realize you're not the same person without your normal habits. This happened to me after four months of working out. My life changed for the better. I started noticing that I looked forward to going to the gym instead of dreading it. I began to have more energy after my workouts instead of less. I was becoming less self-conscious and obtained this newfound energy and love for life. It sounds like I'm making some bullsh*t up, but like I said, it's something you have to experience for yourself.

I was not always like that, though; I used to fear the gym because I was so skinny. I didn't even know how to work out. I constantly worried about being judged by others instead of focusing on my own goals and health. I wanted to change for the better. So, to start, I made a simple goal to go to the gym at least twice a week. After completing my goal for a month, it soon became simple. I then wanted to push myself to work out five times a week. After three months I realized I didn't have a goal anymore. Then I asked myself, *Why not aim high?* Even if I fall short, I would still be remarkable. I constructed a new plan and goal to workout at least 365 days within a 547-day span. This meant that for a year and a half I would be allowed 182 days to rest, and for the other 365 days I was required to work out during those days. Even though most of those days were spent simply on cardio, the truth of this all is that I wouldn't have gotten this far if I didn't embrace working out in the first place. To my surprise I completed this goal with fifteen rest days to spare.

You never know what you're capable of. That is why I keep encouraging you to push yourself even if it's uncomfortable. I didn't know five years ago when I first started working out that I would still be living this lifestyle. I honestly love it even more than I did when I first experienced the change. To this day, I still wake up at six in the morning to work out before I leave for work. I can now walk into work early, every morning, full of energy, instead of waking up last minute and rushing to work sluggish. I do admit some days I don't feel like working out, but that's totally fine. My mindset is programmed to work out a certain number of days a week, and if I miss a day, I will work out on my off day instead.

Don't let small things stop you from living a happier life. Don't tell yourself that you don't have time or that you are too tired. Maybe you don't live near a gym or don't have money for a membership. There are alternatives. The question is, are you willing to do what it takes? If you want to live a healthy lifestyle bad enough, you will find solutions to your problems.

I recently found cheap DVDs and books at a used bookstore that provided multiple workouts. You can do all of these workouts in your living room or backyard. There are also free workouts online if you search hard enough. You can always learn to work out without a gym or money, but we often make excuses because it is easier that way. So, start small and just be consistent. Remember to set goals for your workouts, but do not let them become overwhelming. Remember, balance.

Here are a couple of other tips to help you along your journey. I learned that your body will not change overnight; however, your motivation and patience can. So, during your journey, try not to look at your body every day. It will be difficult, but keep in mind that if you're working hard and eating healthy, then the changes will come. Anytime you start feeling lazy, remember to reassure yourself of how much better you'll feel afterward. Think of your workout as only being thirty minutes, or 1/48 of your day. When you put it like that, you'll feel more obligated to go! Afterwards, you'll have the sense of accomplishment for the day and then you can go back to binge-watching TV without feeling too terrible, because at least you worked out!

Another tip would be to set up a specific day to work out with a partner. Not only will partners motivate you to work harder, but they will also hold you accountable. Next time you think about skipping a workout, your partner will be there to ask you where you were and probably convince you to come! This could work the other way around as well, and you might be the one to motivate your friend!

Most people say working out isn't the hard part, it's the eating healthy part that is. Don't let your workouts go to waste just because you're bored and feel like eating junk food. Try not to eat out too much. Don't try to finish your meals when your stomach is telling you it's stuffed. These were just a couple of tips that will ultimately help you toward your goal. Follow a routine and *stick with it*. If you want it bad enough, you will find a way to achieve your goal.

"If you do the work, you get rewarded. There are no shortcuts in life."

-Michael Jordan

12

THERE IS NO ELEVATOR TO SUCCESS
JUST STAIRS

Wherever you are, look around. How many things have you started but haven't completed? I'm not talking about that half bottle of wine or box of pizza, either. No matter what your goal is, always try your hardest to see it to the end. It doesn't even have to be a goal; apply this concept to everyday tasks. *How you do anything is how you do everything.* My father drilled this concept into my head. At the time, I would become upset or annoyed with him, but now I realize that learning to finish what I started would help me greatly. It's so simple, yet so crucial. At the end of the day, how do you want to feel about yourself? Do you want to feel accomplished, or do you want to feel like you're cheating yourself by taking shortcuts?

When I was young and my father asked me to complete a chore, I would think of the fastest way to finish so I could get back to my video games. For example, he would tell me to take the trash out, and I would, but I never put a new trash bag in the trashcan afterward. He only told me to take out the trash. So technically, that's all I had to do, right?

I'm not even going to try to lie; I failed to finish a task that I started the other day at work. From taking shortcuts while doing small tasks at home to telling myself, *Eh, no one will ever notice* when painting my rental homes. Yes, I've skipped painting little spots in some of my houses because I was too exhausted or hot at the time. I thought no one would ever notice. Then, someone notices the top right corner of the ceiling and I have to go back and paint at an inconvenient time. I soon realized that I was making things more difficult on myself by not finishing what I started. It had become a bad habit of mine. I then saw this pattern directly translate into my everyday life.

When we don't want to finish a job, goal, or plan all the way through, it's because we are being lazy. In reality, we are *so* close to finishing our goals or jobs, but we take the easy way out. Find the energy and drive deep inside you to finish what you started. Here are two tips that help me push past my limits.

My first tip is that every now and then I lie to myself to finish my goals. In no way am I encouraging you to lie to other people. Now, say this with me, "Lying is bad, but lying to yourself sometimes can be good." What on earth did I just say? Basically, keep telling yourself you're almost done, but after you reach your goal, push yourself even more! If your goal is to run three miles a week, then finish what you started and run three miles a week. After you reach your goal, push your limits for one more mile. If your goal is to read five pages of a book a day, then finish what you started and read five pages of that book a day. After you achieve this goal multiple days in a row, maybe try challenging yourself to 10x that goal.

Another tip would be bribing yourself with a little reward. If I asked you to do one hundred push-ups without stopping for $100 in front of me right now, what would you do? You'd probably think to yourself, *There is no way I can do that many push-ups. Who does this guy think I am?* For most people, this would sound impossible and they would decline the challenge. What if after I presented a new offer. What if I told you to do ten push-ups for $10? Do you think that sounds more reasonable? After you did those push-ups, what if I kept offering you $10 for ten more push-ups? Even if you can't do a push up, I hope this example helps you understand my concept. But I'm not saying always bribe yourself with money.

Find simple things that you might not think is a reward. I lie to myself when writing. I tell myself, if I can reach my goal of writing for thirty minutes straight, then after that, I can take a break to use my phone. When I hit that thirty-minute mark, however, I tell myself to write just a little longer, so that my phone will be an even sweeter reward. I usually repeat this process until I'm satisfied with my results and believe I deserve my reward.

It's the same thought process I use even when I work out. I tell myself, *only five more minutes or five more reps. Then I can go home and relax.* I'm not going to overwhelm myself by saying I must stay at the gym for an hour. If your body is exhausted but your mind says otherwise, then you can do it. Kind of like the placebo effect!

How you do anything is how you do everything. To this day, I always replace the trash liner. Since I learned that lesson, I always finish the task at hand. Don't create bad habits when it's so simple to avoid. Don't cheat yourself of becoming great by taking shortcuts in life. Cheating yourself might cause unwanted bad habits to form or even worse, setback.

There Is No Elevator To Success Just Stairs

"It is hard to fail, but it is worse never to have tried to succeed."

        -Theodore Roosevelt

13

YOU ONLY FAIL WHEN YOU
STOP TRYING

Mistakes are okay because that is how you learn. Take that mistake, dissect it, and figure out what you can do to prevent that same mistake from happening again. I can't tell you how many people think that the universe is "out to get them" when something doesn't go their way. Most of the time it is their fault, even when they think that what happened was out of their control.

I knew, some people who would constantly show up late for work and then are dumbfounded when they are fired. They go to their manager and once again blame the traffic, weather, and even other people. They don't take responsibility. They don't think, *"well, maybe it would have been a good idea to wake up thirty minutes early, so I wasn't in a rush to get to work."* Maybe they should have put down their phone instead of updating Facebook or scrolling through Instagram. Perhaps it goes deeper than that, like to the night before, when they were taking tequila shots. They knew they had a huge presentation at work the next morning, but they wanted to impress some friends at the bar. Whatever the mistake he or she made, it is fine if they learned from it. It is not fine if they made this mistake and didn't learn anything from it, or worse, they sit and feel sorry for themselves. It's tough being fired from any job for actions that could have been prevented. If you can't learn from your mistakes, what employer would want you to work for them?

Take a second to think about a time when you thought the world or universe was after you. What are some obstacles you experienced? During those hard times, were you blaming others or taking responsibility for these setbacks? Did you bathe in your own self-pity or did you chant, "I get knocked down, but I get up again" from "Tubthumping" by Chumbawamba?

I'm currently going through a major setback that has devastated me. I purchased a house with my father that needed some serious remodeling. We have already been working on it for a while now because I have limited funds. Furthermore, after purchasing the home we discovered that the house had a lien on it. A lien is a right to keep possession of property belonging to another person.

Possession of that property is kept until a debt owed by that person is discharged. So, we bought this property from someone, whom we trusted at the time, and thought there was no need to do a title check. A title check is an examination of public records to confirm a property's legal ownership and find out what claims or liens are on a property. This lien, that we never saw coming, ended up costing us a large sum of money.

As upsetting as it is, I know this is my fault. Even though I want to push all the blame on my parents, I know that I can't. I must take this error on my part as a lesson and learn from it. Now, I'm sitting here thinking of all the ways that I could have prevented this setback. If I had just taken some time to research more about the property or was more involved with the transaction, then this setback might have been diverted all together. For situations like this in the future, I can confidently tell you this mistake will not happen again. I took my error and learned from it. Retrospectively, I'm glad I experienced it how and when I did. It was a good lesson to learn with just one property instead of five properties later in my life. No matter what, there is always a light at the end of the tunnel if you look hard enough. If you don't see it now, don't worry, you will soon. Just be patient.

"Sometimes good things fall apart so better things can come together."

-Marilyn Monroe

14

THE ART OF
PATIENCE

How much can you handle before you lose your sh*t and say "f*ck it"? That came off a little stronger than intended, so, here is a more socially acceptable way to say it— "The capacity at which one can accept, tolerate, delay, trouble or suffer without getting angry or upset". Learning the art of patience will not only help you in finishing this book, dealing with your siblings, getting through work, but so much more! With enough patience, you could learn anything. Like most skills, however, it takes years of practice to master. In no way am I saying that I'm a master, but these are my thoughts on how I practice patience.

To begin learning patience, you will need to start at the lower levels. The first level of patience is the physical grind and grit of life.

This means understanding that your everyday lifestyle is going to have highs and lows. When something negative occurs in your life, how will you handle it? You should practice encouraging and reminding yourself that you can do this. Whatever *this* is. Whether it is finishing school or saving up money to buy a house. Focus on that specific goal and you will be able to endure any challenges waiting ahead.

The next level of patience deals with your body and mentality. In the heat of the moment, are you going to start flipping out every time something doesn't go your way? Or will you take a step back and think about what your best option is for the sake of your mental health. Maybe that means stopping a fight even when you didn't start it. Usually when tensions are high and someone fights with their significant other, they cut each other off when speaking. Try letting the other person speak his or her thoughts and feelings fully. Then, calmly, find the best solution without causing more damage by retaliating. Is this someone you care deeply about? Think about it. *Do I need to be the bigger person and apologize to end this silly fight?* No matter what viewpoints or evidence you have in an argument, the other person will always be right in their mind. So, what is the point of pouring gasoline on a fire just to be "right"?

My mother used to tell me that my father liked being happy more than being right. He would continuously choose not to argue and would apologize when he sensed an argument brewing. Afterwards, my mother and father would move forward with their day and forget about that dispute. I didn't fully understand my father's genius idea until I got into an argument with my first girlfriend. After that argument, we didn't speak to each other for a couple of days because we both were bull-headed. So, what did this attitude get me? Nothing, and it definitely didn't make me happier.

Even to this day I practice being more like my father. I write these tips to make it seem simple. Even though I practice daily, there are times I still lose my patience. It truly is an art that is tricky to learn. That second level of patience takes years to learn, but ultimately will make life better. How much time could you save or anger could you prevent from learning this level of patience?

The final level of patience is knowing that there are moments in life that are out of your control. No matter what, there are some things you cannot control. This realization is essential. For me, I have lost someone in my life. I don't fully understand why it happened, but it brought the most intense feelings of pain, anger, and sadness I have ever experienced. Even so, it doesn't do any good to place blame on another person or myself. What happened was out of my control and I still am learning how to deal with it.

This next part is tough to explain. I know some of you won't like or agree with what I have to say. But no matter how badly it hurts, just believe that there is a reason why certain things happen. During those times, it is extremely important to be patient. Make sure your emotions don't get the best of you and make you do anything that you can't take back. Express your thoughts and feelings but understand that there are many ways to express them positively rather than negatively. Instead of taking your anger out on a wall or drinking the pain away, like you witness in all the movies, try to be a bigger than it. Go on a run, write your feelings down, or reach out to people. Think about the person you lost and what they would want you to do. They wouldn't want you to place blame or cause harm to yourself.

I know that I can say all of this behind a book. I'd like to believe I could take my own advice when time comes again, but it truly is difficult. Above all, I believe that being patient during an unfortunate event that is out of anyone's control, is the final level to mastering patience. It is something I am striving for everyday and feel like is worth achieving.

Your entire life you will be pushed to your limits. Every single day there will be something to test your patience. Some days more extreme than others. During these times, no matter which level of patience life is asking you to practice, will you remember my tips? If you're on level one, are you going to remember to focus on your goals and remind yourself to stay positive? Maybe it's level two. When something doesn't go your way, can you control your emotions? Or if you're in a fight with another person, will you be the bigger person and apologize so you can go back to being happy? Are you on the last level and recently have gone through a traumatic event? Will you express your emotions in a positive way? Will you go on that run? Will you practice writing your feelings?

SMALL DECISIONS **BIG IMPACT**

INVESTING

"I can shake off everything as I write; my sorrows disappear, my courage is reborn."

-Anne Frank

15

THE CHAPTER YOU WILL
MOST LIKELY SKIP

Writing is extremely important for every person to practice. Great. Now this book is telling me to write. This is probably what you're thinking, but have you ever forgotten why you were doing something or ever wanted to express your emotions completely? Well then, I suggest journaling.

Journals are a way to keep your thoughts, plans, and feelings from being scattered everywhere. Don't be that person who writes down everything on a random piece of paper, only to lose it a day later. I'm sure everyone has gone through something like that and when he or she does this it usually doesn't end up well. I understand writing something down that pops in your mind on whatever is near you at the moment because you're afraid you will forget. However, if you have to do that, at least write it down in your journal later. That way you can keep everything organized in one spot.

With any goals you have, it usually helps to visually see them when written down. If you see your journal daily, you'll be less likely to forget what you have written inside of it. When you visually see something, your brain can process and retain the information much faster. The more senses that are used, the more likely it is that you will remember it. So, write down your goals and plans on how you are going to reach them. Write about something that inspires you, whether that be a movie, person, or business. No, this isn't homework. No one is forcing you to do this, but I *know* it will help.

My mother was the one who got me into writing by gifting me my first journal. Almost every other year she would give me one, and at first, I never used them. I would ungratefully take them and think to myself, *great... another journal.* Then I would toss the journal aside to collect dust.

I always thought of writing as a chore. I strongly disliked writing. There was no time to be writing when I could be doing more exciting activities. Then, as I started getting older, my life started becoming hectic. I noticed that I was forgetting what I needed to do when it came to everyday tasks. No, I am not seventy years old, I am only twenty-two! But these tasks would start piling up and I thought I could contain them all in my brain because, hey, I'm young. Later, there would be this feeling of uncertainty in the back of my head that never went away. *Did I finish that project for work last week?* Other days it would be, *I completely forgot to do all my errands on my day off.* Trust me when I say that life is less stressful and more peaceful after I learned to write things down. That feeling of uncertainty is gone and that's worth the few seconds of me journalism.

I also use journals to write about my feelings. Most of the time, when I'm experiencing deep feelings, I choose not to talk about them. I like to keep them to myself but writing about them helps me. When I write about them, I notice that it relieves a great deal of stress. Writing allows me to relieve this stress alone instead of relying on another person to listen to my problems every time. Another benefit of writing my feelings out would be that I end up understanding them more. When I write them down, my mind really gets everything out. I find out what exactly is making me feel the way I am, and in return, I learn more about myself. Being able to write about my thoughts and feelings consistently has proven to dramatically help my overall well-being. Then after writing I can move on with my day with a clear mind. I have no distractions or wandering thoughts of why I feel a certain way. I have been on both sides. People who do write things down will tell you the exact same thing. The benefits of writing overpower any negative thoughts you could have had against it. People will tell you that they feel less stress, make better decisions, and execute their plans more effectively after writing things down. All this results in being a happier person, which directly correlates with your health.

As Shia LaBeouf's motivating speech goes, "just DO IT". The benefits of writing outweigh any excuses you can make up. A journal can be used for anything you want. Maybe you can use it to write down daily events that happened or for recipes you don't want to forget. Whatever the reason may be, just start writing; you will see the benefits of a clear and organized mind flow into your life. However, do try to avoid writing about negative things. The events you write down should be things you want to come back to or to have peaceful thoughts about. If you were to write something negative, then you're going to reflect on those feelings of negativity. Those negative moments are not worth anymore of your time. You should not write about them because that would mean they are still holding influence and you are focusing on the wrong aspects in life. I'm unsure where I heard this, but I always try to ask myself, was it really a bad day or was it just a bad five minutes that I milked all day? So, practice focusing on the positive experiences you encounter throughout the day instead of dwelling on the negative ones. Write about the puppy you saw or an old friend you spoke to. Journal about how thankful you are to have a healthy body or that you woke up under a roof. There are so many positive things to write about, so why focus on the negative ones?

"Be a rainbow in someone else's cloud."

-Maya Angelou

16

MAKING THE WORLD A
BETTER PLACE

Positive thinking is the backbone to your happiness. Strive to be one of those people that you would want to be around if you wanted to be in a great mood. Those people who attract others because of their positive energy that they constantly produce. As you read that, did you think of someone specific? This person could be anyone in your life; they do not have to be someone you frequently see, either. Maybe it's a family friend or coworker you've known for quite some time. Whoever it is, try to imagine them when you're in a tough situation. What would they say or do if they were in your shoes right now? Would they smile and shake off any negativity? Would they take blame even if an argument wasn't their fault? This person that you're imagining wasn't just born like that. They regularly work on being positive day in and day out because they understand how being positive affects their entire life.

"Is the glass half full or half empty?" You hear this all the time. Nevertheless, some still forget the true meaning of this phrase. This expression is commonly used to measure whether a person thinks negatively or positively. It's all about perspective.

There is a book by Jon Gordon called *The Energy Bus*. It's an awesome and exciting book to read. *The Energy Bus* is all about being positive. One idea from the book talks about how "events + perception = outcome". Sometimes in life we come across events that we have no control over. We often take these events negatively because we don't know any better. We don't know that there is another option other than feeling sorry for ourselves. If you change your perception, you can choose your own outcome rather than letting emotions control you. Imagine if we just chose to be positive more often. I believe that would help everyone live happier.

The Energy Bus also brought the Great Shot Theory to my attention. The term refers to golfing and how we tend to focus on the best shot of the day instead of all the bad ones. I don't know much about golfing, but ask me how many times I've won in mini golf. I can tell you that every time I go mini golfing, I get at least one hole-in-one that I reflect back to the end of the day. Then I make sure that my friends that I went with remember that shot a week or two later. Apply the Great Shot theory to your everyday life and see how it affects you! Instead of reflecting on all the negatives throughout your day try to remember one positive situation that made your day better. I guarantee you'll become a more positive and caring person to be around. Unless you're like me and just gain a huge ego—my friends still love me, though. Your mood won't be brought down because of a bad experience you had that day. You will focus on the positives.

Random acts of kindness will also increase your positivity. It doesn't matter if you're passing by a stranger or family member. Your words or actions can cause a huge impact on others around you. Sharing positivity only makes you a more enjoyable person to be around. Also, when you practice random acts of kindness, this will directly correlate into boosting your own happiness.

Last week I was driving to my cousin's house after a twelve-hour shift. I had been showing properties and contacting potential clients all day in 100-degree weather. I had just pulled onto the highway and I was jamming out to music. I was exhausted, sweaty, and ready to relax. About five minutes on the highway, I saw two cars pulled over in the distance. Next to the cars there was a woman pacing back and forth. She was watching car after car zoom past her while mouthing something. On the ground next to her was a man on his knees trying to remove a car tire. As I approached the cars, something inside me told me to pull over. I can't tell you what made me do it, but I'm glad I did. When I parked the car, the lady stared at me with a concerned look. I opened the door and walked toward them. I threw my hand up, waved, and asked if they needed help. The woman's concerned look slowly faded away as we spoke to one another. As I kneeled next to the man, he stated that he didn't have the correct tools in his car. Luckily, I had the tools they needed in my car. So, I retrieved the tools and helped them change their tire. They were able to leave with their spare on in a matter of minutes. After we parted ways, I couldn't help but smile the rest of the car ride to my cousin's house. It made me so happy to know that I was able to help someone in need. Thursday and Matt, I hope you remember that random Asian person who helped you on the side of the highway. I hope that when you see a chance to help a random person that you do it with a smile on your face.

Here are a couple exercises I noticed positive people practice daily:

1. Try to be more optimistic about life while focusing on the positives as much as possible. Doing this will show you that there is

a lot to be thankful for, which also gives you less time to think about the negatives.

2. Try showing gratitude more often. Even if it's something as simple thanking someone for opening a door for you.

3. Try smiling more. It can make a huge impact on your overall attitude. Sometimes we get so caught up in life that we get used to hiding our emotions—but try to avoid giving out creepy smiles everywhere you go. If something genuinely makes you happy, then smile, and doing so will make you a more grateful person without you even knowing.

4. When you experience something awesome during the day, be sure to share the news with someone! When you tell someone about your experience, you will tend to enjoy it even more. Who knows, it might make him or her smile as well.

Every chance that allows you to practice these exercises, I suggest you try it out! While practicing them, there may be times where other people just won't appreciate you or your efforts. If this happens, simply walk away and don't take it personally. If you take a person's worst day personally, then that will push all the positive energy right out of you. You must understand that there is a difference between staying positive versus bottling up feelings. If you bottle up feelings, it is similar to shaking a soda bottle; when you open it, it's going to explode. People can endure only so much without releasing the tension in some way. What you do with that tension is important to living a healthier life. Don't bottle things up, because it will eventually come out and won't be pretty. Take initiative when life gets tough and figure out what can be done and work from there. Take one step and your other foot will follow. Positive people realize this, so they learned skills to release this tension. It doesn't matter what things are said to them because they know they can handle anything that comes their way. Positive people don't hold any grudges against anyone because they practice daily forgiveness.

"To forgive is to set a prisoner free and discover that the prisoner was you."

-Lewis Smedes

17

SKIP THE E &
LET IT GO

Have you ever been so mad that you did or said something that you didn't mean? If you haven't, then you need to write a book right now and send it to me because you're my hero. I can't tell you how many times I have done or said something out of anger and later regretted it.

Recently I took my girlfriend out to eat and we were having a great time. Little did I know, an argument was forming in the shadows. It started out so minuscule. Suddenly it started blowing up in our faces. That argument then turned into a war in the parking lot. Words were yelled at one another, and strangers stared from inside the restaurant. We both became so upset at the things we said to one another that we didn't talk for the rest of the day. The morning after I couldn't even remember what sparked the argument. I just knew that I wasted a whole night being upset, when I could've been spending that time with her, like I had wanted to. Instead of reaching out to her and apologizing I slept at home the whole day.

Sunday morning rolled around, and I knew I was about to be slammed with work. So, I swallowed my pride and drove to her house, ready to apologize. When I arrived, she was already waiting at the front door with something in her hands. I walked up to her; *she* then apologized and shoved a piece of pie into my hands. We quickly made up, and she told me that I shouldn't have eaten the last bite of her favorite key lime pie. I definitely learned my lesson. And to be honest, I don't even like key lime pie. The moral of the story is *don't eat your girlfriend's food and you'll be okay*. All jokes aside, this whole conflict could've been prevented if I had just been more forgiving during the argument instead of pouring more negative energy into it. Now when we get into arguments, I try to take a step back and think, *is letting my anger get the best of me worth giving up my happiness?*

Silly arguments happen all the time in life, so there are many chances to practice forgiveness. Well, at least in my life there is. Sometimes you might come across a stranger who will upset you in some way. Maybe they cut you off in traffic or were rude to you while in the line to get that delicious Chick-fil-A. The next time this happens, try not to take it personally. Don't hold on to resentment or anger. When you hold on to those feelings, you're jeopardizing your happiness by putting yourself in a cage with grudges. It will eat you alive.

Practice forgiveness every chance you get, and soon you will see how it directly correlates to your happiness. In no way are you forgetting or excusing what someone did to you when you forgive them. You're simply being the bigger person and choosing to be happy rather than dwelling on something small. When an incident like this occurs, just think that there is no way to know what that person is going through. They could have just lost someone close to them or their job. It could be anything. So, try not to retaliate, especially when your emotions are getting the best of you.

Here are a couple tips to try when you feel overwhelmed with negative emotions. If you know the person that might have affected you in some way, try asking yourself why that person would behave that way. If you can somehow relate to his or her feelings, it will help you understand where they are coming from. Sometimes simply understanding where a person is in life will help you control your reactions.

Try not to make yourself the victim in every situation. A victim mentality is a personality trait that is learned when a person is constantly making themselves out to be the victim. If you stop playing the victim, then you will stop blaming others for everything that goes wrong in your life. This will help you release some of those negative emotions that you hold toward others.

Think about a time you were forgiven for something horrible you had done and how you thankful you were to be forgiven. Everybody deserves another chance, and sometimes you just need time away from that person to realize it. Talk to your best friend or family about the situation instead of letting the situation ice over.

Overall, those were just a couple of tips on how to practice daily forgiveness. Take a step back, breathe, and try to listen to what the person is saying. Can you understand or relate to his or her thoughts? If not, then maybe you're just playing the victim role because it's easier than admitting you're wrong. Is this person someone you care deeply for? If so, should you give them another chance? Sometimes you just need to ask yourself this question and let others do or say what they need to. Not everyone will understand your actions or motives. Let these people place limits on you but realize, they don't know your potential.

Skip The E & Let It Go

"If someone tells you YOU CAN'T, they're showing you their limits, not yours."

-Dwayne Johnson

18

THEIR LIMITS
NOT YOURS

"You're going to fail". "You can't do that". Don't let others tell you what is wrong or what is right. Even if it's your friends or family telling you so. Don't let them tell you what to do with your life or how to live it. *It's my life*—wise words of Bon Jovi. No one knows what genius ideas you're thinking or personal goals you're trying to achieve. Even if you fail or fall, at least you're learning and growing.

For those of you who are living in a cave and haven't seen the movie *The Pursuit of Happyness*, there is a scene that I think about when people's words or opinions get to me. It's a true tearjerker moment. I strongly suggest you watch this scene with a tissue to wipe your eyes afterward. Honestly, I just suggest watching the whole movie if you haven't. SPOILER ALERT! The scene presents the main character, Will Smith, with his son on a basketball court. Will tells his son that he doesn't want him playing too much basketball because he thinks his son will be below average, like himself. Will then notices how much he upset his son and realizes that the whole world has been telling him the same thing about his vision to sell his medical devices. He then goes up to his son and says, "Don't ever let someone tell you that you can't do something. Not even me. You got a dream? You gotta protect it. People who can't do something themselves they want to tell you that you can't do it. You want something? Go get it. PERIOD." It's important to have faith in yourself because there will be times when no one else will. Not everyone can see the vision that you have, so do not let anyone tell you what you can or can't do.

If you ever doubt yourself—and you will—just take a deep breath and *know your worth*. When I doubt myself, I do just that. I will take a deep breath and remind myself of my self-worth. Yes, I talk to myself! No, it's not weird or bad to talk to yourself. You're simply circulating your thoughts and clearing your mind. It is just a pep talk, and that's how some of the most remarkable people overcome obstacles. Sometimes if you look close enough while watching sports, you can see athletes talking to themselves too. They are secretly motivating themselves. They understand if they do it enough, it can help them beat whatever it is they are facing.

Maybe they are facing a large deficit in a match, or they are simply having negative thoughts. If they think positive thoughts, it can be a real game changer. It seriously works; just watch Serena Williams play tennis. If she ever finds herself in a tough spot, she will whisper something to herself, and the next point she will turn the tables on her opponent. Those athletes that you watch constantly work on being the best. Part of being your best is knowing your self-worth. Don't you want to be the best you can be?

I'm sure you've done this before but didn't realize it at the time. Have you ever been running and were just about to give up, but pushed a little farther because you told yourself you can do this? Maybe while working at your job, you pushed yourself to finish one more bundle of paperwork. Whatever it may be, think back to those times. Pep talks work, and you know it!

A couple years ago, I used to take everyone's opinion to heart. I cared deeply about what others thought and did my best to please everyone I spoke to. I was afraid of people thinking a negative image of who I was. Now, when I hear other people's negative opinions, and I shake them off. If I believe in my self-worth, then I shouldn't take to heart someone else's negative thoughts.

Instead, use that negative energy and turn it into motivation. It doesn't matter if you have to leave yourself sticky notes or talk to yourself. Just do it.

When I dropped out of college, I remember my aunts and uncles genuinely worrying about me. The most vivid moment I remember was one night when I was having dinner with my cousin and uncle. We had just made it back to the house with some delicious takeout after a long day of work. The three of us were so hungry that we hardly spoke to one another. Then, my uncle broke the silence and asked me, "Why you no go back to college? It's no good to be working without a degree." Maybe it wasn't that Asian, but I do remember it being extremely awkward. I didn't have a response, so I started stuttering nonsense. Here we were, having dinner, and I couldn't even answer his question! Not even in broken English. My cousin, who was about to finish college, changed the subject. I was so embarrassed at the time, but I am thankful for what my uncle asked me that night. I keep that moment in my mind as a constant reminder. I have something to prove, not only to him, but to everyone who told me that I could not do it. I'm not saying that I'm 100 percent positive that I did the right thing, but at least I'm not in college just because everyone else thinks it's the best decision for me.

Experiment with different strategies to remember your self-worth. Figure out which one works best for you, then utilize that strategy every chance possible. Do you need to have more pep talks with yourself? Maybe you need to remember the negative words that people share with you and use them as motivation. Always protect your dreams and goals. Remember, if someone tells you "You can't do it" or "That's impossible," they are telling you their limits, not yours. Now, how will you apply these tips of self-worth into your lifestyle? If you have trouble finding something that works or keep doubting yourself, I suggest finding yourself a mentor to help sharpen your skills.

"A mentor is someone who sees more talent and ability within you, than you see in yourself, and helps bring it out of you."

-Bob Proctor

19

A GPS TO YOUR LIFE
COULD BE USEFUL

Having a mentor is like having a GPS on your phone. Sure, you might be able to direct yourself in the right direction using a paper map, but a mentor knows the quickest route to your destination, similar to a GPS. They also know what problems or stops you my encounter if you decide to take a specific path. You owe it to yourself to find great mentors. A mentor is someone who teaches a less experienced person his or her knowledge. If you're lucky enough to find a mentor, they can help you tremendously.

Before you head off and find a mentor, you will need to identify the type of mentor you are searching for. What do you need a mentor for? Are you in search of someone who has his or her financial life together, or someone who is always happy? Maybe it is a person who is highly advanced in the same field of business that you are pursuing. Whatever the case may be, you will need to answer these questions first or you could end up wasting your time. What do you want to learn and who could you learn this from?

Some of the first mentors you have, whether you realize it or not, are your parents. Seek your parents' knowledge and learn as much as you can from them. How did they do this or that? What mistakes did they make so you don't make the same ones? There is so much to learn and it's all a conversation away. It is too easy to forget how wise someone truly is when we are constantly around them.

I know that in some cases, there isn't someone so accessible to ask, like parents. Not everyone is fortunate enough to have both parents in their life. In some cases, you must literally go and search for a mentor. Mentors have people asking for their advice all the time. You might even be turned down multiple times, but be persistent because this will only help you to grow. If you want to achieve your goals or dreams bad enough, you have to find a way to get the right person's attention. Show that mentor that you're determined to learn from them and that you're willing to give your time and effort into everything. If they can see that fire in your eyes, then they might just give you a chance. Most mentors don't want to teach someone who isn't willing to give 110 percent to what they are saying. So, push yourself, and you might just find someone who will change your life for the better.

Even in superhero movies, the main character typically has a mentor of some sort like Yoda or Mr. Miyagi. The superhero usually needs someone to teach them how to control their abilities and harness their true power. They need a mentor to guide and protect them through those first baby steps. Find a mentor so you can become the superhero you were meant to be!

When a mentor comes into your life, be sure they are someone who can be trusted. Determine if that person is going to have the time and emotional support to guide you. This mentor needs to be able to relate to your situation as well. They need to be able to think back to the time when they knew as little as you do right now. If you don't have a mentor who can remember back to a time like that, then they might not have the patience to guide you. You want someone who understands what you are going through.

I was blessed to grow up with two entrepreneurs as my parents. Without their guidance, I would've never been the man I am today. Even though they teach me new things every day, they allow me to make my own decisions. Whether my decisions are right or wrong, they watch from afar. If I choose the wrong path, then there will be a lesson to learn from it. They understand this and know I will realize my own mistake in the future. If I choose the right path, then they know they taught me well. My parents know, regardless of which decision I make, that it will be fine because they are right behind me. My parents planned out what would happen to me if either direction was taken, and that they were going to be there to support me no matter what. If you can find yourself a mentor, then that is awesome! I can only wish that you find great mentors like all the ones I have in my life. For those who can't find a potential mentor, perhaps it is up to you to take matters into your own hands.

A GPS To Your Life Could Be Useful

SMALL DECISIONS **BIG IMPACT**

"Knowledge is power is time is money."

-Robert Thier

20

STRIVING TO BE BETTER THAN YESTERDAY

No mentor? No problem. No matter how much you know, just remember that there is always more to learn. There are some things that just can't be taught to another person. So, I suggest reading as much as possible to learn as much as you can. There will come a time in your life when no one is pushing you to learn more, it will be up to you to push yourself. You will soon feel comfortable with where your life is, but this is exactly when you need to take the time to educate yourself.

For some, this is the preferred way of learning. My mother is a great example of this type of person. The amount of knowledge she has gained from books is enormous. If my mom wants to learn something new, she reads and reads until she has perfected whatever she was trying to learn.

Take time to read or take a class and learn something new; you never know when you'll be using this new skill or knowledge. If you're lucky, you might even find your purpose in life. The purpose of why you were put on this earth. You might find your passion, something you absolutely love doing. You just never know! That's why I challenge you to continue to educate yourself when no one else will.

In my free time, when I'm not working or spending time with my family, I try to read. Key word is "try". Reading is not my favorite thing to do, but I know that it is a better use of my time compared to playing games or binge-watching Netflix. I always challenge myself to read a chapter from one of my self-improvement books, even when I feel exhausted. That's where some of the ideas in this book have come from. I have picked up ideas from multiple books and decided that the most helpful ones will be fused together in this book right here. So, it's your lucky day. I summed up these books so you can obtain a substantial amount of knowledge from a single book.

If I didn't read any of those books stacked in my room, then this book you are reading would not exist. I know this to be true, and I'm thankful to have taken the time to read them. Each of those books have led me to write all of this. I discovered when reading my self-improvement books that I wanted a book of my own and it didn't matter how poorly written it was. I wanted something to call mine. Try to make reading a healthy habit instead of feeding unproductive ones. In my case, playing video games was my unproductive habit.

Try not to think of your continuing education as a chore. Think of it as wanting to be the best version of yourself. Realize that, if it's your decision and you're doing it for your own personal benefit, you might be more inclined to act rather than wait.

Here is an example of when I changed my perception when I was trying to learn something new. In 2018, I tried to get my real estate license and my mother tried to help me while she also studied for hers. I didn't listen to her at the time because I was more focused on spending my free time with friends. Initially, it was my mother's idea for me to complete a real estate course. It was her suggestion, so it wasn't pressing for me to obtain it. However, after a year had passed, she told me all about the money she made and saved, it intrigued me. After that point, the real estate license changed from being my mother's suggestion to one of my goals.

Receiving my real estate license was a goal that I had to work hard to obtain. I spent my own money to enroll in the necessary courses and took the time to study, read, and experiment with what I learned. The fact that I spent my own money on the courses held me accountable. If I didn't follow through with my courses, then I knew I would be wasting my time and money. This goal wasn't a chore to me anymore; it was a choice to become better than I was the year before.

You have to decide to be better than yesterday, the day before, or even year before. The fact that you are taking the time to read this book is a first step to being better! Continue to feed your brain so you can become the best version of yourself today. Remember, it isn't a chore. It's your choice to be better than you were last year. Continuing education will not only help expand your choices, but also your chances at finding your passions as well. Even though I'm a college dropout, I take every opportunity to expand my knowledge. I also understand that if I want to learn even more, then I must surround myself with people who are aiming for a better future for themselves as well.

Striving To Be Better Than Yesterday

"Surround yourself with people who challenge you, teach you, and push you to be your best self."
-Bill Gates

21

SURROUND YOURSELF WITH
GREATNESS

Have you ever hung out with someone for so long that the two of you started to act like each other? If you haven't thought about this, or don't believe me, then I suggest discussing this idea with your best friend to see what his or her thoughts are on the subject. Jim Rohn stated, "You're the average of the five people you spend the most time with".

I guarantee that some people have never realized how much another person influenced them until they read that last paragraph. I mean, I didn't fully understand this until after I left college.

Who are the five most influential people in your life right now? Are they coworkers, friends, family, or maybe a mentor? Do they support your goals and dreams?

The people around you, do they actually help you to grow? Maybe they are the ones telling you that you can't go after a dream because it seems impossible to them. If you're tackling any of the ideas in this book and start to wonder why it is so difficult, look around you. Are the people around you passionate about achieving greatness, or are they comfortable with where they are at? Do they help or hinder you?

Once you can answer all those questions, you will know what your growth is lacking. Surround yourself with people who are more intelligent, ambitious, and hardworking than you. The quickest way to achieve the impossible is to surround yourself with people who are better than you. Just by being around them and hearing them pummel their goals one after another, will propel you to accomplish yours.

Maybe your goal is to become a writer. I personally know that becoming a writer is hard enough when you are just starting off. Don't make things harder on yourself by surrounding yourself with people who don't share the same ambitions as you.

If my roommate wanted me to go drinking every night, how long do you think it would take me to write a book? After going out enough times, I would probably give up on the idea of writing a book. Waiting too long, I know my ambition would fade away. Contrary to now, imagine if I were to surround myself with people who shared the same interest as me. What if, instead of hanging out with someone who drank all the time, I was with someone who was writing his or her own book? Don't you believe I could finish my book quicker? At the very least it would not be a writer's drunken horror story to wake up and see so many horrible revisions. I could also bounce ideas, thoughts, and receive feedback from this person, instead of passing out on the couch at two a.m. with my drunken roommate.

The making of a book would become my new normal. It would no longer seem impossible for someone my age to write his or her own book. My standards would skyrocket and my ambitions would follow.

Life seems much easier when we are constantly having fun and staying in our comfort zones. People want to have fun all the time. If your friends are constantly going out or partying, then you will do it too. That is because you don't want to miss out on the fun or FOMO. Life like this won't last, though; eventually life and responsibilities catch up to us and hit us when we are exhausted from all the fun. I'm not saying to abandon all the friends you have right now, either. I'm just saying that you need to be wary of who you surround yourself with. Unfortunately, you might realize that some of your friends are holding you back. It may be sad, but I can tell you that I've lost contact with many of my friends because we didn't share the ambitions. If I had not stopped hanging out with some of them, I know that my life would be different. I might have given up certain goals or dreams to fit in better with my friend group. And because of that, I don't believe I would be living the life I would have wanted either. Not that my friends were a terrible influence; we just didn't share the same interests.

Are the people surrounding you better than you? Do they share the same interests as you? Ask yourself these questions, then you will know who or what's best for your life. Surround yourself with people who are goal-oriented and constantly pushing to be better. The outcome of your life will be very different compared to just floating where the wind blows you. No matter how difficult life becomes, we need to remember to trust our struggles and focus on becoming a better version of ourselves every day.

Surround Yourself With Greatness

"If you are going through hell, keep going."

-Winston Churchill

22

TRUST YOUR
STRUGGLE

It doesn't matter who you are, everyone is or will be going through some type of struggle in their life. Struggle doesn't discriminate between gender, race, health, wealth, or anything else. We're all in the same game just at different levels. We're all facing our own battles and demons, so don't be too quick to judge another person by his or her cover. Whatever you're facing, try to remember that there will be a silver lining in the challenge that stands before you. No matter how big the difficulty or how scared you are of it. Whether it is financially, physically, or even mentally breaking you, it will pass. Once you overcome that obstacle, there will be a more understanding and knowledgeable version of yourself.

All struggles are relative. Although I grew up while my family became financially fit, does not mean I did not experience any type of struggle myself.

In my case, when the word "struggle" comes to mind, I think back to the end of my senior year in high school. It was the first day of spring break. All was going well, and I was close to finishing my last semester of high school with straight A's. I was thinking about the car I was going to get, the new one that came with all the beautiful girls. What I didn't discuss was the stress I experienced when spring break ended.

After working so hard for the past years, I told myself that I deserved to have some fun—and then things got out of control. I started experimenting with drugs more and more, until I did too much of something that I couldn't handle. One thing about me is that I'm a control freak, and this drug made me hallucinate more than I ever had before. I lost control of my mind and after a couple hours the situation went downhill. It was the most intense drug experience of my life, and not a second of it was enjoyable. There were hallucinations that I will never get out of my head. I became highly paranoid and felt like something was after me. I started to not trust anyone and refused to eat anything, which only made things worse. I ended up pushing everyone away. The only person I trusted was my best friend, Ben. He did his best to calm me down, but after a couple days, I ended up pushing him away as well.

That weekend at the end of spring break, my parents were out of town. I was at home with my grandmother, who lived with us at the time. She could tell something was wrong and tried to get me to eat something, but it was too late. I was terrified and sleep-deprived from not sleeping for three days that I could not handle reality. I was ready to give up. So, I looked at her and started crying because I had all these thoughts of hurting myself. I went into my parents' bedroom and I wrote them a goodbye note. I placed it on their bed. I looked around for a couple seconds as if it was the last time to see the house. I couldn't think clearly and didn't know how I was going to do it. So, I just walked to my car and drove off.

Somehow, I managed to make it to a highway. As I drove, I gripped the steering wheel harder and harder. The single thought of silence was sounding better as I blocked out the eerie voices whispering in my head. I closed my eyes as I neared a type of turn that with a single misdirection of the wheel would shoot me off into a giant fall. Tears rolled down my face as I placed all my weight into my right foot. Just as I thought it was all coming to an end, my phone started ringing. For a brief moment, I opened my eyes to glance at it. The name that popped up made me smile and forget about the darkness around me. I snapped out of the paranoia for a split second and realized that I didn't want to do this. I slammed on my brakes. My car was stopped in the middle of this ramp with the sun glaring in my eyes. I truly believed that I wouldn't be here writing this if that person had not called me. I thank this person all the time in my head. Unfortunately, I don't talk to them anymore as much as I should.

As I drove home, all these thoughts went through my head. Thoughts of what I almost did. How devastated my family would have been. Thoughts about everything I wouldn't have been able to experience, like raising a child, having my own family, and starting my own business. Then came a random thought about how I left my laundry in the washer for over a week. There was no filter to the thoughts that came flooding in.

After a couple days of forceful eating and plenty of sleep, I soon recovered physically. To this day, however, I can still remember much of what I hallucinated during that time. I always look back on everything that had happened, and don't understand how I let myself get to that point.

When I felt fully recovered, I spent the whole day with my best friend, Ben, in his garage. We conversed about life like we always did. For the first time in weeks, he made me laugh with one of his bad jokes. We talked about everything good in our lives. Everything we had to be thankful for. I remember going home that night, thinking to myself that it was a good day. The instant I put my head down on a pillow I knocked out even with the lights still on. A couple hours later I woke up to a phone call and a familiar voice telling me that Ben had passed away.

My body was paralyzed as I tried to breathe. I thought that this was all a nightmare because I had just spent the whole day with him. The darkness came back in an instant, and I sat there for a second. Watching my mind destroy what I had just thought to be my reality. I thought maybe I was dead, and this was my hell. I thought I was being toyed with by demons and that I really did fly off that ramp. I didn't know what to do. I no longer had my best friend to turn to.

My sadness and fear transformed into anger. I punched everything until my knuckles bled. It took me a long time to realize that he wouldn't have wanted me to go back to that dark place. So, I told myself I was going to be strong for him and to find something positive to focus on.

I found that his family was in as much pain as I was, so I told myself I was going to help them with anything they needed. Helping them made me feel better for a while, but I soon moved away for college and didn't see them as much as I had initially wanted. There were days in college that overwhelmed me, days where I didn't have a chance to think about Ben. Days where I felt sick and thought my memories of him were fading.

I did not want to forget any memories of Ben; I wanted to do more to remember him and make him proud. I knew he would have wanted me to do more with my life than what I was currently doing.

I will always be a stronger person because of our friendship. I dedicated this book to Ben because I never had the chance to give him a book that would change his life like he had done with mine. I truly believe that if I had given this book to him in high school, then we would still be laughing in his garage together.

Life can be tough no matter who you are. Keep your head up and trust your struggles. There was a reason why you picked this book up, and I can only hope that it helps in some way. Even if you only take away one thing, I will be more than satisfied.

-Michael

Trust Your Struggle

SMALL DECISIONS **BIG IMPACT**